R

Happy birthday

from the big

momma Bear!

Gaga—

07-06-05

WELCOME TO THE WORLD OF

Bears

Diane Swanson

WALRUS
B O O K S

Edited by Elizabeth McLean
Cover design by Steve Penner
Interior design by Margaret Ng
Typeset by Tanya Lloyd
Cover photograph by Victoria Hurst/First Light
Photo credits: Thomas Kitchin/First Light iv, 4, 6, 10, 12, 18, 20; Bryan & Cherry Alexander/ First Light 2, 16; Victoria Hurst/First Light 8; Wayne Lynch 14, 26; Robert Lankinen/ First Light 22; Mark Raycroft 24.

Printed and bound in Canada

National Library of Canada Cataloguing in Publication Data

Swanson, Diane, 1944–
    Welcome to the world of bears

    (Welcome to the world)
    Includes index.
    ISBN 1-55110-519-5

    1. Bears—North America—Juvenile literature. I. Title. II. Series.
QL737.C27S92 1997   j599.74'466'097   C96-910734-X

For more information on this series and other Walrus Books and Whitecap Books titles, visit our web site at www.whitecap.ca

The publisher acknowledges the support of the Canada Council for the Arts and the Cultural Services Branch of the Government of British Columbia for our publishing program. We acknowledge the financial support of the Government of Canada through the Book Publishing Industry Development Program for our publishing activities.

Contents

World of Difference

FAT AND FURRY, BEARS ARE HUGE. In North America, they come in three sizes: big, bigger, and biggest.

One black bear can weigh as much as three men. A grizzly, also called a brown bear, can outweigh six men. And a polar bear—the giant of them all—can grow as heavy as ten men. When they rise up on their back legs, grizzlies and polar bears are much too tall to walk through doorways.

As big as they are, bears are light on their feet. They run well, too, turning easily this way and that. Grizzlies can run faster than cars are allowed to travel in towns.

This five-year-old grizzly weighs several hundred kilograms (about 1000 pounds).

1

Furry coats keep polar bears warm on ice. Furry soles keep the bears from slipping.

Polar bears have wide, specially equipped feet. Thick fur on their soles keeps them warm and helps them move on slippery ice. Partly webbed front paws help polar bears swim.

All three kinds of bears have small, round ears and short, stubby tails. But they come in many different colors. Polar bears are white or yellowish. Grizzly bears are mostly brown, gray, black, or blond; many are streaked with gray. Only some black bears are black. Others are brown, bluish, or the color of cinnamon. And as odd as it sounds, black bears can even be white.

Most grown male bears live alone. Young bears, or cubs, live with their mothers for up to three years. When the cubs head out on their own, the moms usually start another family.

THREE GREEN BEARS

Each of the hairs on a polar bear is hollow. Each is as clear as glass. Light bouncing off these hairs makes the bear look white.

But in the late 1970s, three polar bears in a California zoo turned GREEN. Their droppings in the pool where they swam became fertilizer for millions of tiny green plants called algae. Many of these plants slipped inside the hollow hairs of the polar bears, turning them green.

Where in the World

HOME IS WHERE THE TREES ARE—
for most black bears and many grizzlies. But
polar bears live on treeless sea coasts,
islands, and ice.

Rambling around their huge homes,
bears travel far and wide. In a year, a black
bear can wander through about 80 square
kilometres (30 square miles) of forest. A
polar bear can roam land nearly as large as
Lake Huron.

Sometimes, traveling bears—especially
black bears—come close to people. They
check for food in towns, and on ranches
and farms. Bears may even follow streams

The hump on
a grizzly's back
makes it easy
to recognize.

5

These black bear cubs have found a comfy bed — a large patch of soft, thick moss.

and railway tracks into big cities. There they might raid garbage cans and barbecues.

Most bears escape harsh weather by nestling into winter homes — sheltered places — called dens. They often sleep for weeks at a time, not eating, but living on stored body fat.

During other seasons, bears also sleep a lot, especially after eating. To make rough beds, some bears dig hollows in soil. Others flatten bushes or spread fallen branches. Then they flop down for a snooze.

Although there are fewer bears than there once were, black bears still live in much of North America. Grizzly bears live in northern parts of Europe and Asia, and in northwestern North America. And polar bears live in all the countries along the Arctic Ocean.

HOW BEARS CAME

Long ago, many people believed bears were powerful spirits that had come to Earth. Today, many scientists think bears developed from a doglike animal.

About 20 million years ago, bears were likely very small. Gradually, they became bigger and heavier. New kinds appeared, and some old kinds disappeared. Of all the different kinds of bears, polar bears are the newest. They've been on Earth about 100 000 years.

7

World Full of Food

BEARS EAT TO LIVE—AND LIVE TO EAT. They stuff themselves with many different types of food.

Grizzlies and black bears feast on ferns, graze on grasses, lunch on leaves, bolt down berries, and gobble up grasshoppers. With big paws and curved claws, they over-turn rocks and dig into anthills, lapping up insects. And they shovel out any ground squirrels they hear or smell.

Bears go fishing, too. Some hover on shore and whack fish out of the water. Others plunge into streams and snatch fish with their jaws. Above and below water,

It takes a lot of berries to make a meal for a big black bear.

A salmon heading upstream leaps right out of the water — and right into the mouth of a grizzly bear.

they see about as well as you do.

Heavy but speedy, a grizzly may hunt a big animal — a moose or an elk. What the bear can't eat in one meal, it hides under leafy branches for later.

The polar bear feeds on berries, grass, and seaweed. But mostly, it eats other animals. Its long claws are well built for grabbing prey, especially its favorite — seals.

The polar bear often hunts on ice that forms over parts of the sea. It may sneak close to a dozing seal, then pounce. Or it may check the ice for holes where seals bob up to breathe.

Even if snow hides the breathing holes, the bear picks up the scent of seals; its sense of smell is super. It brushes away the snow and waits. When a nose pokes up through a hole, the bear swats the seal and yanks it onto the ice. Time to eat.

Teeth tell a lot about a bear. Long, pointed teeth show that it kills for food. Short, flat teeth show that it also chews plants. A hole in a tooth may show that it eats sweets, such as honey.

Teeth even tell the age of a bear. Layer by layer, they grow as long as the bear lives — sometimes more than 30 years. One layer forms in the teeth each year. Wider layers are signs of good times — of good health and good eating.

World of Words

HUMAN BABIES CRY FOR HELP— AND SO DO CUBS. Whimpering and snuffling are some of the first sounds cubs make. Their mother responds by feeding them and keeping them safe.

As bears grow, they learn about other sounds. A cub that strays may hear its mother calling it back. "Huff, huff," she says loudly. And just to make sure that the cub understands, she may swat it with her paw.

A grizzly bear may guard its fishing spot by "talking" to another bear. It uses its body as well as its voice. Standing tall, it may

"Help!" This black bear cub is hollering for its mother.

13

There's not much fight in a yawning polar bear. In fact, the bear may be trying to say that it's friendly.

growl loudly and swing its head to say, "This is where I fish. Go away." Striking the second bear makes the message even stronger.

When a bear wants to make another animal go away, it may bluff, or pretend to attack. It roars fiercely and charges! Suddenly, it screeches to a stop. If that prevents a battle, both animals are better off. Fighting is dangerous, and it wastes energy.

Some bears make signs that seem to prevent fights with other bears. Using their sharp claws, male grizzly and black bears scratch trees high up. They might be saying, "I'm big, and I'm around here."

But a really big yawn is one of the easiest ways for bears to say they don't want to fight. Sometimes a bear yawn means even more. It can say, "Let's be friends."

GLAD TO MEET YOU

When two polar bears meet, they may walk around one another, sniffing. Then they stop and s-l-o-w-l-y move toward each other. The smaller of the bears keeps its body low. Sniffing again, they touch noses, then nibble each other's necks.

That's how polar bears introduce themselves. When the same two bears meet again, they are not afraid. They may even act like friends, playing or resting together.

15

New World

BEAR CUBS ARE WINTER'S BEST SURPRISE. They are born while their mother is sound asleep in her den.

Eyes shut, the helpless newborns wriggle close to her. They nestle their nearly naked bodies against her warm, furry one. They press close to suckle her, filling their bellies with rich, thick milk.

Now and then, the mother may waken, sniff her cubs, and give them a lick. But she soon falls asleep again.

Usually, there are two cubs—both tiny. Even huge polar bears start life only the size of guinea pigs. But they grow fast. After a

Polar bear twins greedily guzzle milk from their caring mother.

month, the cubs can open their eyes. Soon they are sniffing each other and tumbling around in the den. By spring, they are wearing fluffy fur coats. They are ready to step outside.

Polar bears often have to break out of their den. They push and scratch through snow and ice. The mother bear may

From inside its tree den, this tiny black bear cub peeks out at spring.

carry her cubs out. The sudden light dazzles them.

Like other types of cubs, polar bear cubs don't go far at first. They hang around the den, exercising, growing stronger, and getting used to their strange new world.

When a mother bear of any kind goes off to find food, her cubs scramble after her. If she must leave them alone for a bit, she puts them someplace safe. That may be up a tree or in a snowbank. But she always returns to feed the cubs and keep them warm.

SNUG IN A DEN

Bear dens help cubs stay safe, dry, and warm. Grizzly and black bear cubs snuggle in caves and tree hollows—or in dens their mothers have dug. Soft rugs of grass, moss, and leaves make these dens cozy.

Polar bears make dens up to 3 metres (10 feet) long by digging in snowdrifts or, sometimes, by pushing up ice slabs. With cubs and mom tucked inside, the air in a den can be 20° Celsius (36° Fahrenheit) warmer than the air outside.

Small World

CUBS HAVE TO LEARN HOW TO BE BEARS. Their mother teaches them. She shows them what to eat, how to fish, where to hunt—even what to fear. Bear cubs need so many lessons that they stay with their mothers longer than most other animals do.

Waddling behind her, grizzly and black bear cubs watch their mother closely. When she stuffs herself with berries, they stuff themselves, too. When she scoops honey from a hive, they scoop some, too (or lick the honey off her nose). The cubs practice catching fish and frogs—even grabbing snakes that sun themselves on rocks.

Never far from its mother, a grizzly bear cub checks out a sunny stream.

21

Polar bear cubs follow their mother and do what she does. That's how they learn to live in their icy world.

And whenever there's danger, they learn to obey their mother at once. Her warnings often send them scooting up a tree to safety. But sometimes they climb trees just to catch a breeze. Wind cools the cubs and helps keep flies away.

Not long after polar bear cubs leave their den, they learn to swim. They plunge into cold water and paddle like dogs. When they tire, they climb on their mother's back and ride to shore.

Polar bear cubs also learn how to travel across ice and snow. Lying on their tummies—legs spread—they coast down slopes. And they watch their mother hunt seals, so they can start hunting, too.

When danger lurks, polar bear cubs duck behind piles of snow. They learn to stay as still as ice statues until it's safe to move. Then they head on to the next lesson.

MOM ON GUARD

As big and strong as bears are, they always watch for danger. People and wolves sometimes hunt them, and grown male bears may attack cubs.

Standing on guard, a mother bear rises on her two back legs. She checks for signs of enemies and sniffs the air for danger. If anything threatens her cubs, the hairs on her neck and shoulders stand straight up. Then she charges. To save her cubs, a mother bear will fight to the death.

23

Fun World

THERE'S PLENTY OF FUN IN A BEAR'S WORLD. Playing helps cubs grow strong. And it helps them practice the skills they need to feed, fight, and hide.

Bear cubs pounce on floating sticks, then toss them aside—as if the sticks were fish. Growling low, they chase, box, and wrestle other cubs. One black bear cub may splash another with water or chase it up a tree.

Even grown bears play together. It helps keep them in shape and improves their skills. Mother bears also play with their cubs. And now and then, a grown grizzly plays with a raven. The big, black bird hops

Racing up trees is fun for young black bears. As soon as they climb down, a new race starts.

Play fighting gives polar bears a great workout — as well as a fun time.

closer and closer until the bear chases it. The raven flies off fast. Then it returns and starts the game over again.

In their winter world of ice and snow, polar bears of all ages go skiing. Some stand on four feet to scoot down slopes; others skid on their tummies or their thick back ends. Sometimes the bears ski to get around; sometimes they just ski for fun.

Like other kinds of cubs, polar bear cubs play fight. They waddle around each other before pressing their noses together. One may nibble the other one's ear. Next, they rise on their back legs and start to box.

When the cubs fall over, the game changes to wrestling. But cubs that wrestle in snow soon become snowballs. Then they stop playing to shake themselves—but that's fun, too.

DELIGHTFUL BEARS

Bears often delight people. Here are three good reasons why:

▼ Grizzlies swat at hovering, buzzing helicopters—as if they were flies.

▼ Black bears sometimes fish lying down. They dangle a paw in the water until they feel a fish, then fling it out.

▼ The warm, moist breath of polar bears rises from snowdrift dens, forming tiny, low-floating clouds.

27

Index